Laundry, Laundry

VICTORIA K. HINDS

WESTBOW
PRESS®
A DIVISION OF THOMAS NELSON
& ZONDERVAN

WestBow Press books may be ordered through
booksellers or by contacting:

WestBow Press
A Division of Thomas Nelson & Zondervan
1663 Liberty Drive
Bloomington, IN 47403
www.westbowpress.com
844-714-3454

ISBN: 978-1-6642-0498-0 (sc)
ISBN: 978-1-6642-0499-7 (e)

Library of Congress Control Number: 2020917388

Print information available on the last page.

WestBow Press rev. date: 10/20/2020

Laundry, laundry,

It's piling up.

Some mounds of laundry are soaking wet;

Some are dry and need a folding.

Some are sitting

Scattered,

Molding.

Some are still inside the washer,

Taking extra turns to wash 'em.

Some are spinning in the heat

In the dryer

To a beat.

I don't wanna do the laundry,

But that's what this mama does

Every day, and if I miss it,

Boy, the laundry piles up.

Stuff 'em in there.

Get it done—

Fold them,

Put away again.

That is how it is with kids.

Laundry, laundry,

Never ends!

Let me tell you what I see

With my little family:

Laundry, laundry,

In the drawer,

Rumpled up,

Draped to the floor.

Some are folded,

Some are clean,

Some have dirt stains

On the knees.

Some have tiny holes and tears.

Some are mixed with underwear.

Some go in the PJ pile;

Some are hung in the closet aisle.

Some get yanked out,

Thrown away.

Some get jumped on;

Suddenly,

Some fly over and land on me.

Some will wind up on their heads with

Both arms going through separate ends.

Some will serve as capes and bandanas.

Some get lost

Right in the hamper.

Then there's Daddy's laundry too.

Sometimes they don't look so new.

Some of his go to the cleaners,

Then he wears them out to dinner.

Sometimes Mommy picks them up

When they're scattered on the floor;

Sometimes Daddy's good about it, and

Other times he just ignores 'em.

The youngest child likes to find them

Digging through her

Mommy's drawers.

One by one she pulls them on

Until she can't wear anymore.

Laundry, laundry,
On the couch.
Every day I dump more out.

Sometimes I will leave them there;

Other times I lay them out

And all the stacks start tumbling down

While picking through the mounds of laundry.

Socks that we forgot about
Are put somewhere inside the house.
Once I get them sorted out
I'll match them up, but usually
They won't get matched up easily.

Socks go missing, left and right.

Sometimes I will take my time,

Pile them up until they cry,

"We have no socks, Mom!"

Looking down,

One is blue and one is brown.

Sometimes they will end up wrinkled.

It's okay——just hear me out:

Here's a trick and it's so simple.

Take your iron and throw it out!

Add something wet into the dryer

With the wrinkled shirts and jeans.

Close the lid and get it started,

Spin them till they lose their crease.

Just don't let them sit there please!

I've told them where they need to go.

Every time they change their clothes

I find them scattered on the floor

With several piles rearranged.

I've taught them how to fold them nicely,

How they need to try their best.

They want to help me more than ever,

So we all just make a mess.

Laundry, laundry,
In the stores
Is folded neatly
By the doors.

Stacked up with the stickers showing

Different sizes overflowing.

Some get put on mannequins;

Others hang on shiny things.

Some get mixed in with the others

In different places around the store.

Sometimes it is hard to find

The perfect shirt I'm looking for.

Laundry, laundry,
Still in boxes
That I'm buying on the Web.

Sometimes it is risky business—

Sometimes they're too small or big.

Ties fit gently around the neck.

Boys find them on their father's desk,

Using them to mimic him and

Tying them around their chins.

Dad comes in to tell them, "No,

That's not how the tie should go."

Showing them just what to do,

Then he jokes and does it too.

Some days I am motivated

To stay on top of it and get it done.

Wearing what I wanna wear

And putting away the folded ones.

When dressed up nicely

I look good.

Clothes that fit just like they should,

Then the washer breaks one day.

Laundry, laundry . . .

Go away!

Whoa! It comes back with a vengeance,

Spreading from the laundry room.

Blankets, towels, and teddy bears,

Pillow tops and fitted sheets, and

Hats and pants are everywhere.

And shirts and gloves from soccer meets.

Some I don't remember buying——

It's those kids' from down the street.

Onesies, robes, and jackets too.

Is it good to wash your shoes?

Yes, there's always lots to do.

Our laundry takes up so much room.

I think about it all the time;

It makes me want to lose my mind!

Okay, let's say it——
What if you don't have every luxury
To use machines to wash them clean
Or dry them almost instantly?

What would you do if all you had

Were holey clothes you could use as rags?

What if you washed your clothes by hand

And spread them out to dry instead?

What if you had to make the clothes you wore

Or didn't go into certain stores?

What if this is what you want to do?

What if this was all you knew?

There are countless other kinds of norms.

Not everybody can afford

Clothes right off the runway floor.

Who's keeping track of what I wore?

My life is good;

I'm very grateful

I can't complain where I am able.

I'm overwhelmed

For days on end,

But I'll get through it—

I know I can!

I'm grateful for the clothes I own
And all the layers I put on.
And for clothes I donate to the stores
To someone else who needs them more.

I'm grateful I can buy them too.

I have the choice

To pick and choose—

Wear something old or something new.

I'm grateful that I have a washer;

The dryer runs each afternoon.

I'm grateful also for the water and

Heat to make them feel brand new.

It's good to keep these things in mind.

Sometimes I don't realize that

When I take the time to say

"God, I'm thankful for the day,

For all these things you've given me"

It certainly changes how I think.

I'm thankful for these comfy towels and

For every load that's coming out.

A time will come when they are gone——

No more kids to run around and
No more laundry on the ground.
I'll wish I had more time to spend
Washing all these clothes again.

Laundry, laundry,
There you are.
I'm glad to see you
In my car.

About the Author

Victoria Hinds is a God-fearing, half Hungarian, Midwestern native, who is also a loving wife, and a "Supermom" of six children. She holds a BA in Graphic Design from Upper Iowa University and an MBA in Marketing from University of Phoenix. After completing numerous studies, she used her skills as a Composition/Page Designer at The Geneseo Republic newspaper. In Texas at the Plano Star Courier and at Ad Pages Magazine, Victoria was able to enjoy being a Graphic Artist. Over the recent years, she has focused on taking care of her ever-growing family. The author's experiences have given her an overall unique perspective on life, which she has carried through in her poetry. Victoria's works serve as wonderful sources of inspiration that provide a sense of love, and compassion, and help readers stay connected and present with loved ones, and their surroundings—all to give God all the glory.

Printed in the United States
By Bookmasters